My A

GW00391574

Abou

At the age of 20, Peter's world collapsed when he suffered his first panic attack. Unknown to him at the time, this attack signalled the emergence of a social anxiety disorder - coloured by generalised anxiety and seasoned with panic disorder - that would lead him to hell and back. This is a true story of how he hurtled head first into a mental crisis, triumphed over his illness and how he set himself free. Peter's story offers hope and inspiration to those suffer from social anxiety, generalised anxiety and panic disorder.

1

Contents

One: In the beginning

Two: The bear in the room

Three: The past is a foreign country

Four: If you water it, it will grow

Five: Avoidance is a dangerous therapy

Six: Festival time

Seven: Four walls and a telephone

Eight: The drugs don't work

Nine: Are ok, Mr Fry?

Ten: Out of the darkness and into the light

Eleven: Safety behaviours

Twelve: You are the creator

Thirteen: The enemy within

Fourteen: It's my life

Fifteen: Helpful tit-bits

Sixteen: Useful organisations

One: In the beginning

4.53pm on a summer's day, beer in hand at a friend's barbeque, was the day that I died...or, at the very least, my life was 'flipped-turned upside down' (as the Fresh Prince might put it). My life, before that summer's day, would prove to become a distant memory as I slipped through the gates of hell leaving my saner self behind as a broken figure in the background of my life.

My saner self was an easy going, laid-back character that enjoyed all social aspects of life. Admittedly, perhaps, not the most confident of young fellows by the age of 20, I was never hindered by self-doubt or self-consciousness. It began as tightening in the stomach; a general whole body fuzziness that seemed both strange and alien. Was it, perhaps, the questionably barbequed sausage that stared back at me from the bun that was beginning to feel like a lead weight in my hand? Was it the over exuberant swilling of ice-cold lager that is the preserve of youthful vigour? It was hard to tell at this point. In fact, as my fight or flight mechanism began to whir into action, my naivety of youth responded in the only way it knew – panic!

Whirring from the garden, past the blur of faces that slipped away behind me like star-bursting headlights in a rear view mirror, I found myself lying on the bathroom floor of my friend's house gasping from breath. Certain in my mind that, at this point, I must be suffering from a heart attack or some other type of cardiac event I thought that the spectre of death was approaching rapidly, sharpening its blade and ready to pluck me from the mortal coil. As time passed in the bathroom, the feeling of utter body crippling agony faded and I was left utterly fatigued as if I had run a marathon backwards. Later, I returned to the barbeque as if nothing had happened. And it was at this point that my life would slide into an abyss of social anxiety.

Two: The bear in the room

Many moons ago, in the medical arena, people with social anxiety may have been branded as 'painfully shy' and more of a shrinking violet or wallflower than an outgoing extravert. But social anxiety is much more than shyness. It cripples and disables the sufferer from engaging in everyday social interactions.

The Diagnostic and Statistical Manual of the American Psychiatric Association (APA) currently defines social anxiety disorder as follows:

A. A persistent fear of one or more social or performance situations in which the person is exposed to unfamiliar people or to possible scrutiny by others. The individual fears that he or she will act in a way that will be embarrassing and humiliating.

B. Exposure to the feared situation almost invariably provokes anxiety, which may take the form of a situationally bound or situationally pre-disposed panic attack. The person recognizes that this fear is unreasonable or excessive.

C. The feared situations are avoided or else are endured with intense anxiety and distress.

D. The avoidance, anxious anticipation, or distress in the feared social or performance situation(s) interferes significantly with the person's normal routine, occupational (academic) functioning, or social activities or relationships, or there is marked distress about having the phobia.

E. The fear, anxiety, or avoidance is persistent, typically lasting 6 or more months.

F. The fear or avoidance is not due to direct physiological effects of a substance (e.g., drugs, medications) or a general medical condition not better accounted for by another mental disorder.

If you are reading this, I guess you are someone who suffers from social anxiety or someone close to you is suffering from this mental health problem. If you are reading this on behalf of a sufferer, I will try to crystallise exactly what social anxiety feels like so you can understand it more clearly. For sufferers, you will probably be nodding along as I recount my trials and tribulations with the disorder and how it impacted upon my life.

Most people who suffer from social anxiety fear social situations, but to think as the fear as situational would be a mistake.

Someone who suffers from social anxiety will be anxious leading up to the event, during the event and after the event. They fear that at some point during the event they will say or do something embarrassing. They worry about becoming the centre of attention. They worry about being able to cope and whether they are going to emotionally melt down like a defective nuclear reactor. They worry about how other people will perceive them. They worry about being worried. I'm sure you get the picture... they worry.

They are consumed by worry and this creates a sense of panic that permeates down to their very core. Social anxiety has a massive impact on a person's sense of self-worth and their self-confidence. It invades every aspect of their life extending its tendrils of terror into every fibre of their being. Immobilising, destroying and robbing the person of their life.

Most people who have social anxiety dread every day activities such as: meeting strangers, talking in public, speaking on the telephone, talking to authority figures, shopping, eating and drinking, and socialising. Anything that is social and requires interaction with others, the social anxiety person will dread. In turn, this dread will cause certain body functions to become hyper alert as the body's flight or flight mechanism kicks into action. The body will begin to produce adrenaline and the sufferer will begin to experience a wide range of uncomfortable sensations such as: brain fog, a sense of impending doom, sweaty palms, racing heart, feeling sick and trembling. If the panic builds to such an extent, the sufferer may experience a panic attack which is an overwhelming sense of fear, apprehension and doom, all packaged up with racing heartbeat.

Conventional wisdom suggests that, like most anxiety disorders, social anxiety is a product of a mix of genetic and environmental factors. Anxiety disorders often run in families with children having a greater chance of suffering from an anxiety problem if one or more of their parents have suffered. The science cannot identify the mix of genetics and learned behaviour on the genesis of the disorder, but it has identified that the behaviour of parents can directly affect whether a child will develop a social anxiety disorder. If your parents are worrisome or anxious, then children often learn poor coping strategies when life deals its many stressors. According to the National Health Service (NHS), people with social anxiety often report their parents to be: overly critical, overprotective, not affectionate enough, overly worried about negative outcomes, and exaggerating the idea of stranger danger. Later on in this book, I will be advising you that living your life looking back in the rear-view mirror is definitely not a strategy when successfully overcoming social anxiety. However for the purposes of this book, I will try to pin-point what I feel was the genesis of my own social anxiety problem.

Three: The past is a foreign country

Where did my social anxiety come from? Like the beautiful game, my social anxiety seemed to be a game of two halves divided between my younger and older self. When I was a boy, I grew up in a house that backed onto a wood, and beyond the wood a golf course could be found. Many summer holidays I spent playing in the woods with my friends building dens, sword fighting and climbing trees much to my parents' dismay.

As my friends and I grew into slightly older boys, we ventured beyond the tree line of the woods onto the golf course getting up to all sorts of high jinks that is the preserve of cheeky, young school boys. We hunted for golf balls in the rough and sailed our rubber dinghies across the lake in search of white orbs of treasure that lay just below the ripple of the surface. Sometimes, we would even hide over the brow of the hill on hole nine and when a golf ball came skidding into sight from a golfer's ambitious opening drive we would nab it and flee with the loot clutched firmly in our sweaty hands. I was the leader of our band of brothers and life seemed like an endless play of possibilities.

Was I born with social anxiety? Not that I recall. Was I anxious as a child? The golfers who gave chase wielding their clubs with angry yells wouldn't have thought so. Did my parents err on the side of caution? I would conclude yes. I was born to working class parents in the North of England and my childhood was a largely positive affair.

My parents worked hard and provided me with every advantage they could. In terms of material possessions, as the old phrase goes, I wanted for nothing. Emotionally, my parents were very risk adverse: everything had to be weighed, measured and embarked upon if the risk was not too great. I thus grew up with a rigid mindset that one must work hard, achieve and be unflinching in the face of well managed choices in life. Many would say that these world viewpoints are healthy and harmonious to forging one's way in a tough capitalist society and, to be fair, I would struggle to argue. That being said, I grew up with a strong desire to succeed and a perfectionist mindset.

I was the high achiever at school, top of all my classes and destined for big things. I battled and bruised my way through the academic requirements of comprehensive school with a raft of straight A's and I was ready to fly the nest and embark on a life of success (or so I thought).

After completing school and then college without a hint of social anxiety apart from the quivering hand when engaging in public speaking, I embarked on a university degree at Exeter University. I managed to secure acceptance into an Economics course which required A-level maths which I did not have. Was I concerned I didn't have A-level maths...not really. I was confident that with some hard work and a little bit of elbow grease, which had served me well up to now, I could overcome any hurdles along the way. Bags packed, car loaded and with a sense of enthusiasm and possibility I travelled down to Exeter with my parents to begin a new chapter of my life.

The first 3 months at Exeter University, like any other student experience, was a whirl of parties and drinking games that, although enjoyable at the time, were perhaps not the most productive use of my time. As the partying carried on and intensified, the studying for my economics degree became less and less.

Up until this point, I had been immune to academic hardship: immune to the impending feeling of academic failure that comes with the forgetfulness of the five P's (prior-preparation-prevents-poor-perform). The upshot of this naive and somewhat destructive behaviour was a rapidly approaching point of no return in my studies. There are only so many lectures on accountancy that you can sleep through before the books become unbalanced. And now, it was the end of year accounts. I had made it to six months of study, but I was failing and failing hard. And so the time had come. I left university and returned home to reassess my life and to mentally process failure.

Failure for a perfectionist is a difficult box to uncheck and the conscious and subconscious ruminations in my mind started to fester. I'm not good enough! Will I attain a graduate career? I'm a total disappointment! And so the self-loathing began.

Looking back from my vantage point in life now, I scream at the young man: don't take life too seriously, no big deal, reflect and learn, but unfortunately he doesn't hear me as he wades forward in the darkness of self-pity, blinded by the false logic of worry. My behaviour at the time reminds me of Gollum from *The Lord of the Rings.* As I slip on the ring of worry and self-pity, I increasingly became blinded to my madness and so slipped away my sanity uncovering aspects of my being, whether genetic or environmental, that had lay dormant. In the darkness, the dark passenger, as one fellow mentally challenged human once called it, had awoken. And he was ushered in on 4:53 p.m. on a summer's day.

Four: If you water it, it will grow

After the barbecue, the social anxiety began to fester in the background of my mind. The problem with anxiety is that once it begins it can quickly invade all aspects of your life. And so it did. At the time, I was unaware that I was developing an anxiety disorder.

It's difficult for the younger person, or even adults for that matter, to have the self-awareness and the knowledge of anxiety to accurately assess what's happening to their body and mind. After the barbecue, the anxiety somewhat dissipated and, at any rate, I still wondered if I had suffered a minor heart attack. Worrying as a heart attack might be, I seemed fine and with the unassailable confidence of youth, I continued with my life without seeking a medical explanation for why my body had trembled and shook as the uncooked sausage had approached my mouth. I decided that I would take a year out from university, gain some life skills and go back in the next academic year. With the seeming disappearance of my anxiety, I completed a year of work during which I lived frugally saving up a sizeable nest egg to help me with my tuition fees. I looked forward to going back to university.

The time came to begin university again and this time at a more local university in Sunderland. Living at home did have its advantages and I did think it would keep me from a life of women, wine and song that had led to the demise of my first foray into academia. It was at the commencement of my new degree in history that the anxiety came back full force. Perhaps it was the fact that I was treading the uncertain boards of academia or that I was thrust into a new social circle meeting new people, but my body began to behaviour in strange and particular ways.

Meeting new people became a problem. My body seemed to be conducting its own weighing and measuring protocols of new individuals, but by what parameters I was uncertain. Some new people would cause gut wrenching anxiety to the point where my face would twitch uncontrollably and my heart would feel like a small imploding sun ready to eviscerate everyone around me. While others didn't seem to elicit the same response, they seemed to fall into a seemingly unquantifiable safe zone. People in positions of authority also became a battlefield of emotions and caused anxiety that would send my mind spinning and my body shaking. I remember vividly making the once weekly trips to meet my course lecturer who would check in with me to assess my progress as part of my studies.

Mrs. Whyte was a genial woman with burnished, red hair and an easy manner. She was a calm and assured lady that I'm sure that my internal people weighing system, which I had bizarrely and unhelpfully developed, would rank as non-threatening in any other situation. But as it was, and as it is for people with social anxiety, I might as well have been summoned to a meeting with Satan himself who would cast me into eternal damnation of the weak and pathetic. My mind would become flooded by what ifs. What if I stuttered? What if my facial tics took over? What if I couldn't think of anything intelligent to say? I felt that if any one of these behaviours became apparent my university career would come to a swift and abrupt end.

I can recall vividly climbing the solid-wood stairs up to her office; rubber legged with a sense of dread that pervaded my very soul. Thinking back, apart from being kindly offered a cup of herbal tea in these meetings, nothing of note ever happened. And there's the rub with social anxiety. Nothing ever seems to happen especially not what one predicts or envisages may happen. Satan never appeared. The world never swallowed me up. Yet, with herbal tea in hand, I suffered a torturous inner turmoil that never became any better across the entire three years of our weekly meetings.

I struggled on under a cloud of inner torment, weighing and measuring individuals as I went. Looking back at the time, I was held to the knife point of thinking styles associated with social anxiety that constantly adds fuel to the internal fire that rages away. It was only as I researched the condition and educated myself about the mind that I was able to challenge thinking styles that kept me enchained in a world of social anxiety. Through education and self-help, you can literally change the way the brain behaves, and so it is paramount that we identify the false thinking of a person with social anxiety.

There are a number of areas that intertwine to allow social anxiety to begin and develop. Social anxiety is a complex psychological disorder, but from my experience you can begin to challenge the component parts and, over time, you reduce social anxiety to the point where it becomes less important in your life. In fact, as your thinking skills improve, you can become a person with an above average level of social confidence.

Yes! I did say that! You can become socially confident. If you, like me, and are in the midst of social anxiety, you will probably not be able to believe the prior statement, but it is true and if you complete this book I'm sure that what I have learnt - over many years of suffering - will help you too. You just have to believe it will. You can create the world around you (more on this later!). I will continue to unpack the most important factors in sustaining the anxiety cycle. All of the following strategies that I will talk about and explore are based on Cognitive Behaviour therapy (CBT). When it comes to social anxiety, CBT is a truly effective therapy and it's no understatement to say that CBT saved my life.

Unhelpful thoughts

Unhelpful thoughts sometimes known as automatic negative thoughts (or ANTs, as I like to call them) are thoughts that you have conditioned your brain to believe. You have thought them so many times that you automatically think them - whether you are aware of it or not - in your conscious and subconscious brain before, during and after social engagements. My ANTs ran along the lines of 'I'm weird', 'What if I have nothing to say', 'What if my face twitches' and 'I'm really boring'.

The ANTs would make sure that I was nervous before entering a social situation. Then, as the social situation played out, they would push me towards continuous self-assessment. Was I being witty enough? Was I stuttering? Could people tell I was nervous? The ANTs were thus becoming a self-fulfilling prophecy. I was so involved in internal introspection that I couldn't engage with anyone around me. I probably came across aloof and distant, but at the time I was convinced that how people responded to me was a direct result of me somehow being different and weird.

After the social event, the ANTs would serve up a good dose of analysing my performance always concluding that socially I was an abject failure leaving me thoroughly depressed and dejected. And so the ANTs cycle continued conditioning my brain and therefore my body for anxiety ridden failure. ANTs are destructive and they try and confuse and frighten you at every turn. And there's not just one of them. There are different types working together to try and drag you down and beat you into submission. In this regard, it is important that we understand the sub-categories of ANTs so we begin to challenge and overcome them (more on this later).

It's easy to understand that the ANTs we have can create a world for ourselves that is negative and traumatic. It would be easy if we could simply challenge our ANTs and overcome social anxiety, but it's much more complex than just negative thoughts. Negative thoughts stand beside other processes that keep us locked in a vicious cycle.

Five: Avoidance is a dangerous therapy

A direct product of increasing social anxiety as a byproduct of ANTs is behaviours associated with avoidance. Due to increasing anxiety levels in social situations, the sufferer will begin to avoid said situations or try and escape them as soon as they possibly can. Trying to escape a situation that causes such strong, negative emotions seems like a perfectly plausible method of avoiding discomfort, but all this does is cause the fear to fester and grow.

The next time that you have to attend that party or deliver that presentation you have been avoiding, the anxiety comes back twice as strong. You have effectively told your mind that this is a situation that is dangerous and it can be harmful to your health. Rationally it is not dangerous, but you are telling your brain otherwise. Fear grows and your body's ability to deal with the anxiety decreases. Sufferers thus prevent themselves from experiencing the feelings that the situation will create and they deny themselves the opportunity to prove to themselves that they can actually cope.

For me, my life became a tragic comedic carnival of avoidance orchestrated through excuses to explain my lack of peer participation to others. The excuses had to be varied on a rolling basis to avoid rousing suspicion.

"You fancy a weekend away with the boys, Pete?"

"Err, no I suffer from migraines so wouldn't be able to risk the post drink hangovers."

"You coming to the movies this weekend, Pete?"

"Sorry, I'm a bit skint at the moment."

"Pete, a few of us are going out for a meal after work, fancy it?"

"Sorry, I have to look after the dog."

I didn't even have a dog! There's a saying that goes, 'you have to face your fears and do it anyway'. For the social anxiety sufferer 'facing your fears and doing it anyway' is paramount, but facing your fears has to be done in the correct, graduated way otherwise every time you face your fear – no matter how brave you are – the anxiety doesn't get any less powerful (I'll talk about this in more detail later).

Safety behaviours

When avoidance is simply out of the question, social anxiety sufferers will often engage in a destructive form of misguided anxiety reducing techniques called safety behaviours. People with social anxiety engage in safety behaviours during social activities and at the time it seems to give them temporary reprieve from their anxiety allowing them to 'cope' with the situation.

There are many examples of safety behaviours such as: staying quietly in the background of parties to safe guard against becoming the centre of attention, staying with a louder, more confident friend or drinking large amounts of alcohol to dull the harshness of the anxiety. Did I engage in any of these safety behaviours? All of them! But at the time I didn't know what a safety behaviour was and they seemed like a cherished friend who was supporting me in the darkest days of my life. Standing next to my loud and socially uninhibited friend at a party while quickly anesthetising myself with copious amounts of alcohol, only moving out of his orbit to dish out some broken twiglets before re-docking, I was a poster boy for safety behaviours (how many safety behaviours did you spot in this sentence?) Did I know I was praying at the altar of the safety behaviour? No, and this is what social anxiety is like. It creeps up upon you and like any other bully, it has many tricks in its bag to harass, victimise, bully and brutalise you without you even knowing.

Although safety behaviours help people feel more confident at the time, they serve to fuel the fire of anxiety. They prevent the person from either experiencing the fear and doing it anyway, or being successful in the situation. Consequently, the sufferer feels like they have escaped a fate worse than death and they live to fight another day. They don't get better and the anxiety remains. It is interesting to note that safety behaviours can have secondary impacts such as making the sufferer appear distant to others and this compounds their belief that they are somehow different.

Up to now, we have explored the interplay between ANTs, avoidance and safety behaviours. To overcome social anxiety we need to challenge all these pathways and in the second half of this book I will show you how to put together a raft of therapeutic therapies that will guide your recovery. But before we move on, there is another key pathway that I wanted to mention that sustains social anxiety, internal focus.

When sufferers are anxious in a social situation, their focus becomes increasingly internal rather than external. They tend to engage in a process of self-monitoring. Am I sweating? Is my heart beating fast? Am I shaking? Are people noticing that I am anxious? Is my anxiety escalating? What's coming next? This scrutinising of self is a self-destructive coping strategy that sufferers seem to believe is going to keep themselves safe and navigate the anxiety challenges ahead. Paradoxically, it has the exact opposite effect and actually over thinking causes an increase in anxiety levels. The sufferer will always overestimate how visible their anxiety is to others. Most of the time, people will be totally oblivious to the inner turmoil you will be suffering. Perhaps at worst, you may come across slightly quiet or withdrawn. I have had, in the past, many panic attacks were I would walk out of the room (notice the safety behaviour there) certain that everyone was aware of my emotional meltdown, but pretty much on every occasion no one has even noticed or been aware of my emotional state. 'Pete, where did you get?' they would ask, and I would always have an answer. Deflect them quickly and retreat to pull myself together.

People are simply not aware of others' anxiety and it comes back to the fact that people are not mind readers. Even if people do realise that you are anxious or nervous it never means as much to them as it does to you. The more we check in on our internal processes during social occasions the worse our anxiety becomes. Plus, if we focus internally then we do not fully participate in the social occasions around us. This makes it more difficult to join in and we feel more different to everyone else. Internal focus is another weapon in the arsenal of social anxiety.

Six: Festival time

As they say, hindsight is a wonderful thing. When I was in the depths of social anxiety, I had no idea that I was constructing my internal world by the rules and diktats of ANTs, avoidance, safety behaviours and focusing on the enemy within. And so my life went from bad to worse. And again, strangely, a barbecue was involved.

I had struggled through my second degree at Sunderland and went on to complete a Primary Education Degree at Sunderland University. I am sure you are wondering why someone with social anxiety would embark on a career which relied on standing in front of a group of people and opening your mouth and actually speaking. It was a strange choice of a career, but people below the age of 11 seemed to pass my internal weighing and measuring system coming out the other end clearly labelled as safe people.

It wasn't easy, but with a concerted effort to force the anxiety deep down I could do it. It was difficult, but hey, my life at the time was a pulsating ball of anxiety...nothing was easy...quite frankly my life was awful. That being said, panic attacks and anxiety wreaked havoc on my early teacher training days which often culminated with me vowing never to return to the classroom.

I stumbled and fumbled my way through the course existing on a daily diet of nerves and I was slowly becoming overwhelmed. Finally, I secured a pass and even secured a job to start in September. In celebration of my new found career, I decided to attend Leeds Festival with my friends.

Leeds Festival, for the uninitiated, is a music festival that takes place in a country park in North Yorkshire, England. Thousands of hedonistic music lovers descend on mass to enjoy a weekend of music and alcohol. Occasionally, this festival takes place in beautiful sunshine where one can frolic around the venue soaking up the rays. Mostly, given the temperament of the weather in 'God's Own Country' (as Yorkshire is affectionately known), it's a mud soaked affair which demands sturdy Wellington boots, copious amounts of baby wipes (for mud spatters) and a trustworthy tent. The weather that day was overcast and grey and the clouds looked on ominously, but the music doesn't stand on ceremony and so I grabbed my rain coat and all other festival apparel to see me through.

Bag packed and car loaded, I set off for the festival preparing myself for a memorable experience in good company. The first day and night was an excellent affair with convivial banter and merry libations which concluded with crashing into the tent at some ungodly hour of the morning: a standard weekend for the 20 something young male. The anxiety was there, but I was rolling with it and it was somewhat manageable.

The next day began uneventfully with a morning wash with bottled water and clearing the camp site of the previous night's revelries. And then the barbecue began. Perhaps it was a cosmic joke that barbecues would sign post the story of my life with social anxiety or simply a strange coincidence of experience, but the anxiety began to grow. And grow it did like an evolving creature dragging its way from the primordial sludge birthing itself horrifically into the world.

Looking back on my younger self, I can now conclude that the anxiety of beginning my new teaching job the following week was perhaps the main catalyst for my uncertainty of mind at the time. My GP would later tell me that anxiety often rears its head at times of major change in a sufferer's life. Should I have not gone to the festival? Should I have not placed myself in such a social situation when I was anxious about beginning a new job and all the uncertainty that brings? Possibly, but if it wasn't this meltdown it would have been another. The sign post had been erected and I commenced my journey down the rabbit hole. How deep was it? I was about to find out...

The anxiety slowly grew as the day proceeded onwards. Later, we headed into a local village to have a pub lunch. Before we flagged down a taxi, we were accosted by a young man in a day glow t-shirt and a pharmaceutically enhanced verbosity which seemed to grotesquely contrast my escalating anxiety. I began to withdraw inside myself immediately as I knew anxiety wise I was already on a sticky-wicket. He was a font of energy and unrestricted by the good-old British social etiquette norms of over-familiarity. Inviting himself, he jumped into our taxi and off we went.

I vividly recall the taxi journey to the pub. As Mr. Day Glow became increasingly animated in the taxi with his conversational repertoire knowing no bounds, increasingly my heart raced and my body shook; I was not quite certain at that point what was happening to me as I had never experience a panic attack of this magnitude before. Feigning an absent interest in the world as it slipped by the taxi window, I prayed that none of the party in the taxi (especially Mr Day Glow) engaged me in conversation. I was terrified of being exposed; terrified that my weakness and madness would be laid bare for all to see. The journey seemed to last forever and although I wished for Mr. Day Glow's attention to somehow bypass me that was not to be. He had tractor beamed in on me peppering me with questions and statements for the whole journey.

When we arrived at the pub, all traditional and quaint, I scampered to the loo like a terrified rabbit in the headlights. Splashing water on my face had little effect on tempering the tempest that raged within. I cursed myself in the mirror for being weak; another futile attempt. And so I did what seemed like was my only option left to me at the time. I locked myself in the cubicle and prayed for the world outside to disappear. At the time, I had no tools in my tool box to defeat the social anxiety and so there I remain on the cold, hard toilet seat. How long passed before I emerged from that cubicle? It could have been minutes or hours, but emerge I did.

My emergence was not a beautiful moment where someone conquers a personal challenge certain in the knowledge that they have exercised grit and determination. I was no Edmund Hilary conquering Mount Everest and placing my flag of human endurance in the powdery snow. From the chrysalis of the loo, I didn't emerge as a beautiful butterfly. I emerged a broken man. Mentally fatigued and physically spent, I managed to make my excuses (for my sins, I used the dodgy sausage one again) and I staggered back to the camp site on foot. Bearing in mind that the camp site was 4 miles away, I arrived back at my tent two hours later which taking into account the rubbery legs and the heaving by the side of the road was quite an achievement in my physical state. Unzipping the door of the tent, I climbed into my sleeping bag and sobbed as the sounds of festival song and laughter drifted over my tent.

The next day I had, like many times before, partially bounced back and I held my broken psyche together as we travelled home while I fluffed and plumped up my 'rogue' sausage story to my friends which was more than enough of an explanation for them. When I arrived home, then my problems really began.

Seven: Four walls and a telephone

Although I arrived home without my friends knowing the true extent of my breakdown, I was not the same person as when I had left for the festival. I was changed: I was a worse version of my former self. I had descended down the hole of social anxiety into a darkness that was all encompassing and inescapable. Beating a hasty retreat to my bedroom, my world began to shrink exponentially like a black hole entering my life pulling in both matter and anti-matter. I was constantly shaking and having up to 30 panic attacks a day. If the phone rang, I would have a panic attack. If the door bell chimed, my heart would race into action. If my parents knocked on my door, my fight or flight mechanism activated and I would panic suck oxygen from the air like it was a finite element on the precipice of extinction. Obviously, I could no longer hide this truly horrific ailment from my parents and so I confided in them.

The problem with social anxiety is that often family and friends who have never suffered from it, in my experience, find it difficult to understand. How do you explain to people that you have panic attacks when someone wants to talk to you? It is incredibly difficult to communicate to a non-sufferer and to this day I still think my parents didn't understand, and still don't, what social anxiety is. In my case, my dad was pretty pragmatic suggesting that I should see my GP with great urgency and my mum agreed with him. The problem was that I now couldn't step foot across the door of my home without my body convulsing with panic. I was now trapped in that catch 22 where I needed help, but I simply couldn't access it. And so my agony went on day after day.

My parents grew increasing fractious and my anxiety simply fuelled theirs and the cycle went round and round like a broken, evil merry-go-round. The relationship with my mum became increasingly strained. "Eat your toast," she commanded, as I forced toast down my dry, constricted throat (eating had become a problem). "Pull your socks up," she sobbed through tear-filled eyes. The final, and perhaps most devastating comment to my broken psyche, was delivered through her cutting comment that shook me to the core. "He's just like Uncle Mal."

The first memory of Uncle Mal was the smell of Brazil nuts and tobacco on his large, wrinkled hands. Mal was my dad's brother and he lived at my grandma's house. My dad had often told me Mal had been an enormous hit with the ladies when he was younger renowned for physical strength and his debonair personality. He seemed exotic and intoxicating, and he always had an interesting tale to tell. Under his bed, which was a small box room in the back of my grandmas three bed terraced house, he kept a suitcase that always enthralled me to its contents. One day he allowed me to peek inside. What was this secret stash under his bed? It seemed so important to him and so it was so important to me.

Upon opening the battered leather case, the contents turned out to be his prized collection of Spaghetti Western's that he had been collecting on VHS tape across his lifetime. They were all in there: *The Good, the Bad and the Ugly*, *Once Upon a Time in the West, For a Few Dollars More, The Great Silence* and what seemed like hundreds of others. On my boyhood point system on what made adults cool, Uncle Mal had just smashed an ace. Not just any ace, but a great whopper right down the centre line.

That summer, we watched Spaghetti Westerns back to back causing grandma's old VHS player to draw its last breath: a fitting end to the machine as it sang its last swan song. As time went on, I began to wonder why a cool uncle in his forties lived in grandma's spare bedroom. I was old enough at the time to grasp the social etiquette of not asking Mal directly, but the question continued to niggle away at my eager young mind; after all, he was so cool. I approached my father, "Dad, why does Uncle Mal not have his own home."

Shifting in his seat, my father replied. "Mal doesn't see Trish [his wife] or his kids anymore because he has been unwell. We used to work down the pit together, but one day he couldn't get on the bus with the other men. He was too scared."

Too scared? My young mind couldn't quite seem to believe what I was being told. After all, Mal was so big and strong. "What do you mean too scared?"

"See Pete, Mal suffered from the nerves. It became so bad that he couldn't work or look after his family. Couldn't even go and get a haircut. He turned to the drink to try and sort his problems out, but he just stopped caring, you know. Later, when it got real bad, he got tablets from his doctor but tablets never work. He eventually ended up in Durham Hospital where his brain was electrocuted. When that didn't work, he had to stay in a special hospital for a long time; wasn't the same afterwards."

Dad wasn't one to dress up the truth and there it was...the answer to the enigma that was Uncle Mal in all its ugly glory...but I still had questions. You see, I was a bit of thinker and I still am (perhaps a component part of my anxiety problem). Soon after, I found myself trying to find out what Uncle Mal had endured.

At the time, I did what any young man would do, I waited for the dead of night and, flashlight in hand, and I crept out of my bed and tip-toed over to my computer in my bedroom. I pressed the on button and my Packard Bell desktop computer clanked and cluncked into action and the old 56k modem sent off ear-splitting beeps and peeps into the still night air. This wasn't going to be quick. This wasn't going to be quiet. But I desperately wanted to find out what happened to Mal in that hospital; it was worth the risk of being caught. I found myself reading up about electroconvulsive therapy (ECT).

The use of ECT started out as a series of experiments conducted by scientists in the 1930s when they began to notice that severely depressed patients would notice an improvement in their condition when they had been subjected to this course of therapy. Passing a large electrical current through the patient's brain caused a seizure, and so they hoped, this would reset the brain to a more helpful equilibrium.

By the 1960s – just in time for Mal - this course of therapy was widely used in the UK to treat severe depression. But just like the closure of Britain's mental asylums and the cessation of lobotomies to cure metal problems so too has the aggressive therapy of ECT been decreasingly used. Less aggressive forms of therapy, such as the wave of antidepressant drugs introduced in the 1970s and 1980s, gave doctors new avenues to explore. But still today, ECT is still used for severely depressed patients with circa 4000 people annually in the UK undergoing ECT.

Many doctors, however, are sceptical of this form of treatment suggesting the risks outweigh the benefits with people reporting: memory loss, slurred speech, personality changes and problems with basic mental skills. Opponents of the treatment claim that patients can enter into an addictive cycle where the therapy is repeated often and that any improvement beyond the short term can be due to an extreme placebo effect. The fact that Uncle Mal had endured this treatment with noticeably – to family members – deleterious effects, was difficult to comprehend.

Dad's revelations – that Uncle Mel had under gone ECT and had been sectioned - hit me like a thunderbolt and it was a memory that, throughout my life, I would never be able to shake. Like Oliver Wendell Holmes once said, 'A mind that is stretched by a new experience can never go back to its old dimensions.' This discovery about my uncle would, in time, have a direct impact on my own mental daemons. And so as I struggled to eat my toast, and my anxiety grew, I became a prisoner in my own home...the memory of Mal swam around my head. It permeated my waking thoughts and sleep offered no respite as I awoke from slumber in full blow panic, my bed sheets dripping in sweat. How long until I was pumped full of mind bending drugs? How long until I was strapped to a gurney with faceless doctors placing a bite guard into my frothing mouth? How long until my brain was fried with electricity? How long until I was sectioned? How long until I lost myself forever?

Eight: The drugs don't work

As my mental and physical condition deteriorated, so did my life around me. Eventually, I came to the stark realisation that I was at a point of my life where I 'do or die': I had long since passed any sort of elastic limit and my situation was critical. I was having multiple panic attacks daily, I had become agoraphobic and I wasn't eating due to anxiety. The dark passenger had consumed any vestige of my saner self and I was in free fall. If given the choice to pass away quietly in my sleep, I would have taken it gladly at this point. I would have even said thank you. It would have been a sweet relief.

With the support of my dad, I managed to summon the mental strength and leave my house and make my way to my local GP. I remember passing through my front door which had, in my mind, become an impenetrable portal that was the last line of defence against certain death. Like a vampire, the sunlight burnt my eyes and scalded my skin as I stumbled through the impenetrable portal hunched over. I was a Morlock entering the world of the Eloi. With my dull grey-to-white skin, red eyes and unwashed flaxen hair, I no longer belonged in the world of the beautiful creatures. With jangling nerves, I arrived at the GPs' surgery.

Sitting in the waiting room was like waiting to be beheaded for crimes against the state: I was certain that the executioner, with sharpened axe, was waiting for me to dole out the last and final punishment. When I entered the doctor's room my dad did most of the talking which was rather helpful considering I was ready to pass out at any given moment (perhaps I should take a moment to thank my dad for getting me to that appointment, without him, I cannot even begin to consider where I would have ended up). The doctor, whose face and even gender I can little remember, mumbled something that included the phrases 'panic attacks' and 'acute anxiety' (interestingly social anxiety was never mentioned) and prescribed me citalopram and beta blockers and sent me on my merry way. Slightly relieved I still had my head and that I was not being carted to the nearest mental institution I began to pop the pills to still my tortured mind.

Before I begin to describe my experience of taking medication to treat social anxiety, it will be worthwhile to briefly explore the drugs available from UK GPs at the current time for social anxiety.

Anti depressants

The newer antidepressants which are called Selective Serotonin Re-uptake Inhibitors (SSRIs) are often prescribed for social anxiety as a first port of call. SSRIs work by increasing the level of the chemical messenger serotonin in the brain. Serotonin is a neurotransmitter that is posited to have a calming and mood boosting property on the brain. SSRIs are normally taken via tablet with the lowest possible therapeutic dose prescribed. The dose is then increased by the GP in accordance with the patient's need. The effects normally take two to four weeks to manifest with mild negative effects (agitation, sleeplessness, increased anxiety) in the early stages. Short term negative effects normally wear off as the body becomes accustomed to the changing levels of neurotransmitters.

If SSRis don't help, then Monoamine Oxidase Inhibitors (MAOI) are sometimes prescribed. These older class of antidepressants have draw backs such as lowering blood pressure making the user feel faint. They are used less frequently when compared to SSRIs as they can have dangerous interactions with certain foods and so require dietary restrictions. Also, MAOIs can interact with some over-the-counter medicines such as cough syrups which also can cause dangerous interactions. There are now new MAOI drugs called Reversible Inhibitors of Monoamine Oxidase – A (RIMAs). These drugs don't have the same reactions as

MAOIs and so people who take these drugs don't have the same dietary worries.

There are perhaps two other main drug types when it comes to social anxiety that are worth mentioning, tranquilizers and beta blockers. Tranquilizers, like Valium, were, in the past, used to treat a range of anxiety disorders. But as they are addictive drugs, they are a poor and ultimately dangerous choice to treat someone who has long term social anxiety.

Beta blockers, on the other hand, are well tolerated by the body and can be taken relatively safely over the longer term. Beta blockers help reduce or even remove the physical symptoms of anxiety such as shaking and heart palpitations. Although beta blockers do not affect the mental symptoms of worry, they do stop people from manifesting physical symptoms and so they have become popular with people who have to perform in big occasions such as musicians and sportsman.

I recall a news story about golfers taking beta blockers to help them win tournaments. Mac O'Grady, a former US Tour professional, said that the players taking drugs have won a "bunch of majors...you see these guys meandering around for years doing nothing and all of a sudden they're making all the putts and winning tournaments. Beta-blockers are not illegal. They just make a remarkable difference. They affect the part of the brain which controls fear and anxiety."

And so I was loaded up with my prescription medicines, the SSRI, citalopram, and a course of beta blockers. How did I do? Would I recommend medication as a solution to social anxiety? On one hand, I would answer yes, I would recommend medication, but on the other, I would say no. Let me explain. When I first started to take citalopram, the short term side effects were bad albeit manageable. I had sleepless nights which were punctuated by the most horrific, lucid dreams. Strangely, my ability to climax during sex began to diminish although my performance stayed at its normal level. Initially, my increased staying power was a boon for my then partner, however, this side effect soon became irksome and mildly distressing. But sometimes with medication certain trade-offs are necessary depending on your current state, and to be fair sex was a low priority on my list.

During the first few weeks, I felt drained but eventually these side effects gradually scaled back. The beta blockers made me feel invincible when I was public speaking which at the time was one of my biggest stressors. In presentations, I was immune to the shakes and the racing heart as the beta blockers performed their function amazingly well. I began to feel like a social terminator as I said hasta la vista to the nerves and delivered pitch perfect presentations with wit and va-va-voom: an orator of repute I had become. Over time, after completing the short course of beta blockers and the longer term course of citalopram I felt great. I was returned to a past version of myself which was confident, outgoing and articulate. I was engaging in everyday life and enjoying family and friends around me. The medication was superb and it pulled me back from the desperation of not being able to leave my home. I could now engage with the world around me, but there was a problem.

Medication for social anxiety and panic attack sufferers can literally save lives in the short to medium term and for me possibly it did, but they didn't solve the problem in the long run. Medication will not tackle the under lying ANTs that cause the anxiety. It will simply mask them; it will keep them quiet until the meds are no longer there. Further, when you come to rely on medication it can potentially undermine your confidence in handling social challenges by yourself (remember the safety behaviours we discussed). The problem of social anxiety is that it will often return when a sufferer stops taking medication. If you are currently taking medication, there is no need to stop but for long term change you must learn how to make the psychological changes in your brain that will change it forever. Many experts suggest that taking medication in combination with psychological treatments is the best course of action to facilitate long term and sustainable change. In my opinion, taking medication at the start of your journey to recovery is a great way to give you the initial strength to deal with the problems in your thinking, to begin to identify safety behaviours, to locate your avoidance activities and work on your ability to focus externally all of which are root causes of your social anxiety.

Nine: Are ok, Mr Fry?

Upon leaving my trainee teacher course, buoyed up with my medication, I accepted my first job in teaching at an outstanding primary school. The school, where I secured employ, was renowned for having an excellent academic record for its pupils. I knew it would be a cauldron of hard work and overworked teachers who would be struggling under an education system that was seeing teachers leaving in record high numbers at the time citing poor work-life balance. But I felt confident. I felt ready. I nailed the interview process which was a gruelling whole day affair which saw 20 candidates competing in a gladiatorial round robin interview process. Candidates either passed or failed rounds of testing with the failures frog marched out of the room. Only the strong would survive. This was the nature of the school: it was the nature of the beast. But I was super-charged. I was 'beta blockered' up. The beta blockers were still having the effect of making me feel like the T1000, I couldn't fail. Group debates with the other candidates...no problem! A grilling by the board of governors...bring it on! Talk for ten minutes about an unseen topic that you were given 2 minutes to prepare for. Two minutes, why wait – I'm good to go! Suffice to say, I got the job.

At the time, I felt that my life was on an upward curve. I started my new job but things soon started to go wrong. First, the class I had were an exceptionally challenging bunch. The cohort was filled with children with global learning disorders, autism, ADHD, and a range of other social and emotional disorders. As a teacher, who now has ten years under his belt, this class was a nightmare for the Newly Qualified Teacher (NQT) especially a green around the gills NQT like me. Next, my medication was scaled back on the request of my GP. At the time, I still didn't have a great deal of knowledge about social anxiety and so the ANTs began to creep back into my thinking causing my anxiety to resurface.

The problem with teaching is that children can sense blood in the water and if there is a chink in your armour they will exploit it. Like a shark, they can smell the blood from miles away even before you are aware of it; there were 33 baby sharks in my room. There is nowhere to hide in a classroom and you have to be the pack leader or others will try to take your position. And so the likely boys and girls started to poke their heads up.

The children who loved to swing on their chairs began to swing on them a little more. The children who enjoyed pencil throwing during lessons threw their pencils more frequently and with greater gusto. Children carefully walking to the carpet for quiet-time were replaced by children rolling head first onto the carpet scattering the easier going, cordial children across the room like skittles. Lessons that involved hideously dry topics like the life and times of St. Bede, which you could pull off at your most strongest and most robust, became battle grounds of learning.

As the behaviour deteriorated, the levels of my social anxiety increased. I wasn't sleeping. I was shaking like Bambi on ice when moving around school and my ability to carry out my job was compromised. I went from outstanding lessons to lessons that were just about adequate. Perhaps in a less rigorous and gladiatorial school, I may have escaped under the radar but, as it was, my flagging teaching was quickly picked up upon.

During an NQT year, teachers who simply don't cut the mustard are labelled as failing and are relatively easily shipped out by the management team. In turn, the management team increased their monitoring of my practice and conducted their well versed stress increasing tactics so I would come to the self-realisation that this was not the right school for me. Three months into my new career I handed in my resignation without kicking up a fuss. My resignation was readily accepted, and I left. The social anxiety had defeated me again and left me broken and dejected. The future seemed bleak, a landscape without hope...but I plodded onwards like a wounded soldier.

After leaving my first teaching job, I spent a year on supply. It was a difficult year both at work and in my social life. Supply teaching, for somebody with social anxiety or anybody for that matter, exposed me to the worst aspects of teaching.

Often, but not always, classes were tough going and energy sapping. 'Our teacher lets us do this!' 'I sit next to Billy when our teacher is here!' My anxiety was in overdrive and I would regularly have sizable panic attacks on the way to teach each day's new class. I would struggle through lessons anxious and uncertain in which of the myriad of ways my body would betray me. Would it be the facial twitches or the wobbly legs, which would be worst today? I cannot blame the children in the ways they sometimes behaved as I must have seemed like an unusual specimen at the front of the classroom, shaking and quivering in my boots. I continued with the medication, but the problems persisted.

Outside of school, my relationships with friends factored down into going out once a week on a Saturday. The format of the day consisted of the same activities with me dancing to the beat of the anxiety drum. I would go out in the afternoon and watch the football or cricket. I would stay quiet in my group of friends hoping that I would not become the centre of attention. I would suffer under the pressure of our shared banter which consisted of witty back and forward exchanges sending each other up. I would get self-conscious, shake, stutter and panic my way through these exchanges that everyone around me found highly entertaining.

What others found relaxing, I found horrific. My overriding thought would be, what is the earliest time I can frequent the bar? When could I, without rousing suspicion, secure my first pint and let alcohol work its dark magic?

I had, through my struggles with anxiety, figured out that if I drank a little I could partially quell the anxiety inside. If I drank a lot, I could totally remove it. This logic led to many Saturday nights and Sunday mornings more drunk than any man should be (notice the safety behaviour that I choose to hold in high regard at the time) stumbling through the streets of Sunderland howling and cursing at the moon.

Somewhere between quite drunk and very drunk was my optimal zone for socialising without anxiety, but the problem was I could never quite hit that zone, and I mostly staggered right through it. My friends were then given a dual presentation of myself on one hand as a shy, awkward person and someone that, when drunk, was larger than life. It was not surprising that they responded to this behaviour as slightly odd. And if I had to guess, that is probably how they saw me for a long time... slightly odd or maybe a little shy and repressed. Do any of my friends know I have had an anxiety disorder?   No they don't...or at least I think they don't.   They just saw me as quiet or slightly aloof or in some instances as an arrogant, self-centred bastard. For example, some of my good friends had their stag dos in far flung destinations, but the thought of getting on a plane or even being around my friends in an untested environment give me panic attacks. The mere thought floating across the front of my mind of going on holiday caused nauseating anxiety.

I thus had to create an excuse such as 'I suffer from migraines' or 'I just can't handle the hangovers' so I could engage in avoidance (there it is again another self-defeating coping mechanism). There I was going out and getting blisteringly drunk on the weekends, but not being able to do this same function on a stag do for a good friend.   During my twenties, I was neither good friend, nor a reliable one. Girlfriends were more difficult to hide the anxiety from and so the anxiety would often have many regular damaging impacts on these interactions as well.

The damaging impact of my condition continued to haunt me, but I plodded on surviving from one day to the next in a world which seemed hostile and threatening. I completed one year on supply and was offered a job in a new primary. With an increasing knowledge of my profession, I was finding teaching easier: I knew what to expect and things seemed generally less stressful. I could manage the job and the anxiety at the same time. It wasn't easy, but I could do it as long as I could accept that life was a joyless battle. What else could I do? I accepted life as it was. I didn't know any different.

At the time, I was on no medication and began to build confidence in the work place. As the years past, I became an outstanding teacher and I carried out all my professional duties. Strangely to me, I had become a well respected member of staff amongst colleagues and parents; my anxiety, although still there, was less debilitating. I still couldn't go on weekends away with my friends and the yearly presentation I had to give to parents to introduce them to their new class teacher could only be completed with one of my beta blockers (safety behaviour! I still didn't know this at the time). I had stock piled some beta blockers away for any state of emergency. At any rate, I could see glimmers of light in the darkness for the first time in many, many years. I even began to imagine a life with a 'normal' level of social anxiety, but I wasn't there yet. There were still so many aspects of life that were too challenging. I decided to take action, and it was this action that would lead me out of the darkness and into the light.

Ten: Out of the darkness and into the light

It was when I discovered 'cognitive behaviour therapy' (CBT) that I placed myself upon the path of recovery from social anxiety disorder. The pioneer of this modality of treatment was an American psychiatrist named Aaron T. Beck. Beck developed a theory of depression that was based on emphasising the importance of people's depressed thinking styles which kept the problem going.

In recent years, the techniques that Beck pioneered have been merged with other behaviourists to become a body of therapy know as CBT. CBT is one of the most important methods of overcoming social anxiety. Firstly, CBT has been rigorously tested by scientists and has been shown to be highly effective in people with anxiety problems. Secondly, people who have been treated with CBT or CBT and medication as a dual therapy have been shown to be less likely to have a reoccurrence of the disorder later in life. Thirdly, it has become increasingly clear to psychologists that thinking styles or should we say problems in thinking styles lead directly to anxiety. CBT challenges these thinking styles and creates new ones which your brain will begin to use automatically (when practiced correctly).

The problem with CBT is that it is not readily and widely available to the sufferers in the UK. If we try to solve social anxiety ourselves, we can often make the problem worse. In the rest of this book, I am going to bring together all the best practices in CBT that I have learned from engaging in CBT through self-help and in a therapeutic environment. The following CBT therapies allowed me to banish my social anxiety and in fact develop a greater than average social confidence. I now have very little problems leading teacher training seminars, conducting presentations and engaging with others. CBT has given me the thinking skills to make social anxiety irrelevant in my life, and I'm sure that if you invest time and energy in the next section of this book you too will be able to put an end to your suffering. I know the following techniques work because they worked for me. I have done it. Most importantly I have lived it.

ANTs

ANTs are thoughts that create anxiety within. Anxiety doesn't happen in a vacuum; it requires a thought to light the touchpaper to get it going. ANTs create anxiety in that they activate neural pathways that cause the body to respond and to release stress chemicals which in turn generates anxiety. For example, if you tell your brain that spiders are inherently scary and you repeat this thought often enough you will condition your brain to react accordingly when you see a spider. You heart rate spikes and your muscles tighten ready to run away from the danger. This fight or flight mechanism is an evolutionary facet of humans that meant we could survive the threatening factors in the environment. Should a dinosaur appear, your adrenaline surges and you run away from the danger. Conversely, if we tell our brains enough times that spiders are not scary and there's nothing much to fear when we come across one, our body will not behave in a panic stricken fashion. We thus create the world around us with our thoughts and feelings. Such is the power of thoughts on our bodies that they can literally cause death.

For example, take the idea of the cultural belief of voodoo which can lead to psychological stress, illness and death. Walter Cannon, an American physiologist, was one of the first people to write about the fatal consequences of voodoo. In 1942, reports came flooding in from around the world about voodoo deaths. Condemned by medicine men, South American Tupinamba men died of psychological fright. Hausa people in Niger fell to the ground and expired convinced they had been bewitched by voodoo. In

Australia, Aboriginal tribesmen upon seeing an enemy pointing a hexed bone at them, went into convulsions and withered away. According to Cannon, voodoo death was real: "It is a fatal power of the imagination working through unmitigated terror." Whatever you tell your brain, it will believe. You can literally brainwash yourself, and the problem with social anxiety sufferers is that we have brainwashed ourselves into negativity. Is meeting new people really scary or is it only scary to those that have convinced themselves it is?

ANTs are negative thoughts that colour the world grey and make us respond in an anxious fashion. ANTs are conscious and subconscious thoughts that we have conditioned our brains to believe. The trick is being able to identify these thoughts and challenge them. Sometimes, it can be difficult to even identify these ANTs especially when they have been running around our mines unchallenged for so long.

How to spot an ANT

ANTs are tricky creatures and it is imperative that we can identify them and challenge our negative thinking bias. Essentially, ANTs inhabit defined categories and you might have problem with one or two categories or if you were like me you might have all category coverage. Once you become more adept at spotting your errors in thinking, you have taken a giant leap against ANT kind. You are beginning to place the nails in the coffin of social anxiety.

Catastrophising

This style of thinking is when you think any mistake or minor negative outcome will be a total disaster. You think that things will play out with the worst possible ending and these thoughts will often prevent you from doing whatever is frightening you. Such thoughts might include: 'If I forget my words, it will be awful'; 'If I don't get this right, I will lose my job'; 'If I can think of something witty to say, she will hate me'.

Mind reading

People with social anxiety often make the incorrect assumption that they know what other people are thinking in any given social situation. Wouldn't it be great if we actually had that ability? It would, I'm sure, make us social butterflies, able to respond with accuracy and sophistication to every single person we meet. The problem with mindreading, from a person with social anxiety perspective, is that we make negative assumptions about other people's beliefs as we filter external stimulus through our own negative frame of reference. For example, we believe that people think we are ugly or that we are boring.

Often, I would assume someone not paying 100 percent attention to me was because they obviously thought I was dull and annoying. I really didn't know what they were thinking; maybe they were thinking about which condiment they were going to accompany their evening meal with. In retrospect, my misguided notion that I could read the mind of others compounded my low self-esteem and fuelled my social anxiety.

Taking things personally

People with social anxiety tend to take things exceptionally personally. For example, feedback in the workplace can often feel like a hammer blow against one's personality. Perhaps you have a friend that seems unusually quiet during a conversation. A social anxiety sufferer often believes their friend's low mood is a direct response to something that they have done or said. Sufferers often construe comments or actions of others to be a direct attack on their core personality which leaves them anxious and depressed.

Taking the blame

Taking the blame is where an individual blames themselves for something they really can't control. For example, your partner becomes angry with you so it MUST be your fault. If you think about it rationally, you cannot really control other people and they make their own choices about how to behave and react.

Focusing on the negatives

After completing a social occasion, no matter how successful it has been, the sufferer tends to focus on all the negatives and pays little regard to the positives that took place. For example, I used to give public presentations as part of my university course often in front of 50 plus people. Shaking bones and beating heart, I delivered presentations often mentally collapsing after the ordeal.

My mental process consisted of dissecting and unpicking every small pause I made in the presentation, ruminating over my fast heartbeat and wondering how weird I must have looked.

I was certain all the glum faces in the audience were a direct product of my shaking fiasco of an attempt at public speaking. Never once did I congratulate myself on speaking up in front of 50 people and thus I never became any better. No matter how many presentations I completed, every time was as brutal as the first because I had not changed ANTs thinking.

Emotional reasoning

This is where you feel that your internal feelings are a true reflection of the world around you: for example, 'I feel so embarrassed right now so everyone must know this' or 'I feel so uncomfortable right now so I must be making others uncomfortable'. Remember that ANTs never tell you the truth and it's better to tell yourself a more realistic thought and focus away from your inner turmoil on what is happening around you. Stay away from emotional reasoning as you will become locked in an internal struggle while events unfold around you.

Over generalising

Assuming that because something went wrong once, it will go wrong every time. For example, you panicked during a meeting so every meeting will cause panic or because you said the wrong thing on a date you will always say the wrong thing.

Wishful thinking

People allow this ANT to creep in when they start thinking in 'ifs'. 'If only I was more clever'...'If only I was more sociable'...'If only I was wittier'...'If only I was like everybody else'. ANTs love wishful thinking because you are fighting and struggling. It gives them power over you to control and manipulate. Remember, what you resist persists.

Predicting the future

People with social anxiety tend to spend a great deal of time predicting what might happen in the future. Predictions are often based in negativity and predict some sort of future calamity or embarrassment. Rather than letting things happen naturally, the predictions make us worry about what ifs. 'What if I stammer?' 'What if I go red?' 'What if I have nothing to say?' A great deal of time and energy are spent procrastinating and worrying with the final outcome being that you are stressed before entering the feared social situation.

Labelling

'I'm useless'...'I'm boring'...'I've nothing worthwhile to say'...'I'm crap at public speaking'...'I'm not as clever as others'.

Challenging ANTs

When you have an ANT such as 'I hate public speaking', you must challenge it in your brain and then redirect your mind in a more healthy direction. Remember, your brain believes everything you tell it. If you say something is horrible, your brain will act upon it. If you tell your brain something is unmanageable, it will be. You have to challenge ANTs. For example, 'I don't like public speaking, but maybe it'll be better than I thought'. In this way, you are saving yourself the anguish of frightening and scary thoughts by offering yourself a realistic alternative. As long as you give your brain a realistic alternative, then your brain will, over time, come to believe to it.

Being realistic is an important part of challenging ANTs in that you can't tell yourself that you are going to become the world's greatest public speaker when you arise from your bed that morning. It doesn't work like that, your brain won't believe it, but consistently challenging ANTs in a realistic way will cause noticeable changes in the way you respond to social situations. One of the best ways I found to deal with ANTs was to learn coping statements by heart so that when anxiety did strike my coping thoughts would already be there, right in my subconscious mind, ready to combat the ANTs. Memorise the following statements, or sing them from the top of the stairs or write them down until they are etched in your brain.

I feel a little uncomfortable now, but if I focus away from these thoughts I will be fine.

I have felt anxiety before... so what...no big deal.

Anxiety used to be scary, but I can cope better now.

I've done this before so I can do it again.

I have anxiety, but it's like a mirage in the desert. It's not real. It has no power over me.

Also have a few statements ready for when anxiety hits you hard such as during a panic attack. It is very difficult, I have found, to think rationally during a panic attack and so if you have these statements well practiced and honed they should jump to the forefront of your mind automatically.

I have anxiety now, but if I focus on my task, my anxiety will go down.

I accept the feeling of anxiety and it's no big deal.

This has happened before and if I relax it will pass. It's no big deal.

Oh here it is again, I'll just play dead and it won't have any power to hurt me.

It is important to tell yourself that ANTs have no power over you unless you believe them. They are bullies and like bullies they will try to scare you into their way of thinking. But like bullies, if you ignore them and refuse to listen to their lies, their power over you will diminish until they will no longer be a part of your life. Refuse to let them magnify fear. Ignore them. Challenge them and they will die.

If you were like me, you may have had years of ANTs swimming around your mind unchecked and unfettered. At the beginning of challenging ANTs, it is important to remind yourself every day that ANTs are liars and they are trying to deceive you. When you become certain in your mind that ANTS are lying bullies, you can scale back your efforts in telling your brain this fact and continue to practice your coping thoughts.

Practicing your coping strategies will thus prepare you to deal effectively with anxiety. When I was in the depths of my anxiety, I employed many counterproductive strategies in a misguided bid to quell the anxiety. The idea of dealing with the anxiety in a gentle but dismissive way didn't occur to me and I'm sure it wouldn't occur to the majority of sufferers. The feelings are so strong and so powerful that you feel that you too must react in an equally powerful way. Would you enter a duel with a toothpick when your opponent is wielding a Valyrian steel sword that would partition you in two without a whisper of effort? But defeating anxiety is a paradox.

With my anxiety, I always battled it...resisted it...bemoaned my situation...cursed myself for being weak and I became aggressive and hostile with myself. The ANTs greedily fed on my approach and became engorged; my social anxiety escalated. Whatever you resist persists. The only way to defeat ANTs is by being calm, assertively refuse to believe it. Offer your mind alternatives, look upon it as an unwanted friend that you have grown tired of. Never allow ANTs to have any power over you because realistically they don't.

What to do when anxiety attacks

As a social anxiety sufferer, I know that when a panic attack raises its head it's a challenging thing to deal with. See what I did there? If you did see the minor adjustment I made, well done. I could have said that when a panic attack raises its head it's 'awful', 'debilitating', 'terrible' or any other super negative synonym, but I would have been allowing a sneaky ANT to invade my thinking and actually make future panic attack attacks more likely and worse. I identified the ANT and made a more realistic and helpful statement which goes along the lines of when a panic attack happens, it is challenging, but I can deal with it. It would be much better to say that panic attacks are hard to bear, but not unbearable. With ANTs you have to call them out and be more realistic.

In this way, I have already begun to ratchet down what a panic attack actually means to me and over time this causes the body to react in a more helpful way when an attack does arise. So what do we do for the time being while we are working towards removing our ANTS? Again defeating panic attacks - like so much with social anxiety – is a paradox. You might think that fighting the attack and trying to force you anxiety deep down will work. You may flee the room which would remove the anxiety causing factor (avoidance). You might panic. You might let ANTs run riot. The way to defeat panic attacks in the long term is to face the symptoms, however challenging, and do not run away. Accept your feelings and do not fight them.

Observe your anxiety as an interested observer, but don't engage with it; don't react. The adrenaline will tell you to run; it will scream it at you. Stay still and slow down; refuse to react and panic. Consider the analogy of a jelly fish. You are swimming in a beautiful sea and a jelly fish drifts into you field of vision right below you. If you listen to the first voice in your head and panic, thrashing you legs around and flee in haste it, will wrap its stingers around your legs and brutally sting you multiple times. If you stay calm and relaxed, the chances are the jelly fish will pass you by and you can continue with your swim. Anxiety loves it when you fight and struggle. It fuels its fire. When I had to first provide staff presentations at my school, my experience went something like this. I would be plagued with ANTs thoughts days before the event. During the presentation, I would fight the anxiety and try and force it back down. I fought the anxiety with anger and frustration. After the event, I would berate and beat myself up for days that I was so weak for not being able to control my feelings.

Then I began to change. I began to challenge my ANTs before the event. During the event, I would not react to my anxiety I would just remain still and use some helpful coping statements. I would treat the anxiety as an interested observer would. The less I fought the easier it became. Change came slowly at first, but the more I practiced the easier it became. Eventually, I built up so much confidence that I even began to enjoy giving staff presentations (I know strange!). I had become empowered by the simple idea that 'what we resist persists'.

Once you become more adept at spotting ANTs and challenging them with more rational statements and you are confident that if anxiety does strike you have some well rehearsed coping statements to take the pressure off, you will begin to feel more confident and stronger. Like you, I reached this point and it took me awhile to find new challenges and pathways to continue my recovery from social anxiety. Hopefully by me explaining my journey, it may save you time and energy on your journey.

For me, once I had developed my internal resilience through being able to change my ANTs using rational coping statements, the next challenge was to use these thinking skills and to tackle avoidance. As I discussed earlier, alongside ANTs we have other pathways keeping the anxiety burning and avoidance is one of them.

Avoidance is not doing something because you know that in the past it has created feelings inside you that you have convinced yourself are terrible and unbearable. There are many kinds of avoidance ranging from the easier to spot ones to the ones that are sneaky and work away in the background hindering your journey to recovery. My overt types of avoidance centred on not attending parties (if I knew I couldn't drink alcohol), refusing social invitations, avoiding public speaking and not talking to people who I felt to be 'socially' intimidating.

Overt examples of avoidance - once you know about avoidance - jump out at you and smack you in the face. They don't bother hiding and exist in plain sight loud and proud. Some types of avoidance, however, are more subtle and it's important that you identify these types too. For example, these subtle forms may include: not starting conversations at parties; skimming across the surface at social engagements; finding other things to do at parties like menial jobs so you don't have to talk; always doing things with a friend rather than alone. In the short term, avoidance makes you feel safe and for me, I always thought it helped me navigate the trials of life. However, like ANTs, avoidance will lie to you and keep you locked in a vicious cycle of anxiety and it must be challenged at every step.

So how can we tackle avoidance in a sensible way? The first step is to identify what you avoid. Don't be afraid to make a list of these things that you avoid doing. Next, identify the link between the ANT and the event and begin to challenge the ANT with more realistic alternatives. Then, face the fear rather than running away. Finally, evaluate objectively what happened when you faced your fear. Did you actually die? Did you perish? Was it really that awful (remember don't lie to yourself)? Let me unpack these steps with an example of my own to show you how I did it.

When I reached the tackling avoidance stage, I sat down and wrote a list of things I avoided in a hierarchical order from number ten being the thing I least feared, but still avoided, to number one which was the thing I most feared and most definitely avoided. I believe that number ten at the time was talking on the telephone about problems I had with home services. I would almost have a panic attack if I had to ring Next Home Shopping and complain about a delivery that hadn't arrived. I would stutter and stammer my way through the whole conversation. It's not easy for someone with social anxiety to express opinions and tell others how they would like to be treated; it's much safer for us not to kick up a fuss.

At number one was presenting to groups of adults. It is perhaps not surprising that I feared any type of public speaking when we consider that surveys put this fear at the top of the list ahead of the fear of disease or dying. But I would go to extraordinary lengths to avoid it. I would lock myself in lavatories. I would quit jobs rather than do it. I would select modules on my university course that specifically had no requirements to deliver presentations. I would feign injury and illness. I would sell my soul to the devil, and not ask for my change. If I could conquer this fear and the rest on my list of avoidances, then I know I would be cured.

Once the list was written, shaking pen and all, I moved onto step two. I identified the thoughts that went with the activity so let's start at the top, why not! My thoughts about public speaking went something like this: 'I will clam up and everyone will think I'm weird', 'What if I shake?', 'What if I stammer and stutter?', 'What if I have a panic attack and have to run off stage what will everyone think of me', 'I'm not good enough', 'I feel terrible so it will be terrible', 'I panicked last time and so I'll do the same this time'. Can you spot the ANTs at work? Can you spot the errors of thinking (catastophising, emotional reasoning, predicting the future, over-generalising). I had ANTs throwing the biggest party ever in my head. A veritable Mardi Gras with the little blighters banging their diminutive drums (but ever so loudly) and trumpeting their horns. These thoughts went unchecked and unchallenged for years. I had conditioned my brain to believe them to be facts that were etched in stone. I never thought to challenge these thoughts. Why would I, they were the truth, weren't they?

And so I started to generate possible alternatives that ran along on more rational lines such as: 'public speaking isn't my most favourite thing, but maybe I'll do a better job than I thought', 'This fear is like a mirage in the desert, I will keep on walking forward and I'll be fine', 'Public speaking isn't really that bad that's just an ANTs thought, 'No big deal', 'Who cares?'. It's okay to say something is difficult if it is difficult. You can't lie to you brain and tell yourself it will be a walk in the park if it's not. The trick is if you are going to say something is challenging you simply follow it with a but: 'Giving that speech will be tough but I'll probably do better than I thought'; 'Going out for a meal has been tricky in the past but I'm getting better and better at it'; 'Going to the supermarket has been challenging in the past but I'm not the same person anymore'.

After I had began to drop down rational alternatives into my brain which were believable (notice I didn't just say to myself I'll wake up tomorrow and be an amazing orator of worldwide repute), I moved onto testing, facing these fears with my new thinking skills. I started to pick up public speaking again bearing in mind that I had already successfully completed the other 9 things on my list. Success breeds success. Don't just jump straight in at number one; it will be too much too soon. Your recovery is a ladder of success and every rung needs to be climbed methodically and with purpose.

At first, I was anxious when I began public speaking after years of avoiding it, but I was kind to myself; I was rational. I told myself that after years of psychological self-torture that it will take time to get better, and I had been successful just because I did it. Never doubt yourself. Never second guess yourself as this is another ANT weapon trying to keep you rolling around in the mud.

As time went on, I continued to drop rational coping statements in my brain and presentations became easier and the anxiety became less important and so less strong. Sometimes I had to complete, as part of my job, really big presentations to groups of people once annually and for these I always took a beta blocker.

At the time, my girlfriend who knew about my social anxiety suggested that I try to do the presentation without a beta blocker. What? Are you crazy! Even though I had made massive progress, I thought she must be mad and before I knew it the ANTs were back and the self-doubt returned. That being said, I decided to conduct an experiment and, alongside my rational coping statements, I decided to test out these fears. The next week, I didn't take a beta blocker and I completed the presentation. And it went great! It was perhaps my finest presentation I had ever delivered and I received a standing ovation.

Afterwards, I went back to the steps of recovery and evaluated my experience. It was clear that I was relying on safety behaviours by taking a prescription medicine to complete the presentation. When I didn't take it, I proved to myself that it was only an ANT's thought that was trying to convince me of a false reality. I could cope. I did cope. I had built inner strength. This example perhaps serves to demonstrate that no matter how much knowledge you have, subtle forms of avoidance and safety behaviour can sneak in and you always have to be vigilant. See every challenge as an opportunity to build inner strength.

After I stopped taking beta blockers, my inner strength soared to the point where I can now give presentations with a minimal and manageable amount of nerves, in fact I really enjoy them. It would be unrealistic to tell yourself that you want to be free of nerves when doing presentations and having a manageable amount of nerves before a big social occasion is part of the human condition. It is perhaps more important to show yourself that you have the strength to cope with anxiety when it does come along.

When you change your behaviours and begin to tackle avoidance, you are literally taking more risks. Taking risks can initially be scary as you may be worried about making mistakes or doing something that you think others may look upon negatively. It is important to get into the mindset that making mistakes really doesn't matter in the grand scheme of life. Will anyone remember what you said at the party in a year's time? Will people remember that presentation in ten year's time? Will people remember every word you said? The answer to these questions is, who cares?

Everyone makes mistakes and if you think it is only you, then challenge that ANT. Most mistakes people make are hardly ever noticed by others. Mistakes might mean a lot to you right now but they don't to other people, so do more things. Be a social scientist and conduct social experiments and reflect on them at the end. Begin to break the vicious cycles of social anxiety.

When it comes to breaking social anxiety cycles by changing behaviour and not avoiding, it is easy to give up. Progress will be slow at first, but always make sure you applaud your achievements. Watch out for ANTs sowing the seeds of doubt in your mind. The process is not easy and I know this. If it was easy, you would have done it by now. If it was easy, it wouldn't have taken me years to find the correct therapeutic path. But if you believe you can get better, you will as long as you are resistant and persistent...and never give up! Congratulate yourself on successes however small. Get in the habitat of giving yourself a mental pat on the back when you achieve something social that you thought you might never do.

Here is an example of progress I made and how I congratulated myself. For a long time, I would find an excuse not to go abroad as I was terrified to go on a plane. Growing up, I loved going on holiday but that all changed when I had my first panic attack in my 20s. I couldn't get on a plane as I was terrified of close quarters socialising and also I was terrified at the thought of having a panic attack 10,000 feet up. 'Would I pass out?', 'What if I become the centre of attention because of my nerves', 'How would I be stretched off the plane if I passed out'.

After I had begun my CBT and I worked my way up the list to number 3 which was going on a plane, I decided to conduct an experiment and go on holiday. What better reward than overcoming my fear than sipping cocktails from a coconut on a sandy shore. And so I did it... was I nervous?...a little...did I die? no....did I drink cocktails from a coconut?... hell yes! And so I congratulated myself; notice the difference between the negative thought of old and the new, more rational one.

Old thought. 'Anyone can get on a plane.'

New thought. 'I have found this

difficult in the past, but I'm different, now I will go from strength to strength."

Old thought. 'You were still anxious.'

New thought. 'I was a little anxious, but I dealt with it...no big deal. It will get easier and easier'.

I congratulated myself as for me I had come such a long way. To others getting on a plane is no big deal. Does that matter...of course it doesn't. To me it was a big deal and sitting back on my hotel balcony I watched and listened to the sights and sounds of the city and I took the time to say, 'Well done Pete, you deserve it.'

As you continue to improve and congratulate yourself, you will continue to build inner strength. But there will come a day when you have a setback. Setbacks are normal and should be seen as a sign of progress. You are challenging yourself to things that you have found very difficult in the past and so the old neural networks that you have conditioned to fire a strong anxiety response will be still there, but these pathways will change the more you use calm and positive thinking. Changing the way the brain reacts through changing thoughts and behaviours takes time, but the brain can change and it will.

The human brain is not fixed, it is plastic, and so if you have taught your brain to think in a unrealistic way you can equally teach it to work in a rational way: it just takes time and effort. Along the way, everyone should expect and accept setbacks, but take them in your stride. Use your rational coping thoughts to put these setbacks into perspective. Some days you will be tried or unwell and not on top form. 'I was anxious when I met the client today, but no big deal. It's normal. Who cares?' The only way the ANTs will win is if you totally give up and go back to believing their lies. If you have made lots of progress, this progress cannot be lost to one bad experience.

Your brain will remember the more rational and realistic pathways you have been creating. Chalk it up to experience. If you do not give up, you will overcome social anxiety in the end.

Eleven: Safety behaviours

Taking risks, being ever ready for social experiments and trying your best will move you towards overcoming social anxiety, but when engaging in these new ways of doing it is important to also overcome safety behaviours.

Safety behaviours, like popping pills, will sabotage long term progress even if you are working on your ANTs and tackling avoidance. Safety behaviours are things we do in social occasions that we believe, quiet wrongly, protect us from threats. In the long run, they decrease our social confidence and prevent us from building inner strength. When I used to use safety behaviour during social interactions, they gave me the impression that they were keeping me safe and protected. What the safety behaviours were actually doing was preventing me from realising that I could actually cope in the situation. For example, I used to stay on the periphery of conversations not really engaging as I didn't want to feel the anxiety in my body and I didn't want to embarrass myself by saying something stupid. Although I can't read minds, I more than likely struck people as quiet or even aloof. If you behave in a certain way, then people will react to you accordingly. If you don't put out much into the world, you don't get much back. My safety behaviours were thus working against my progress.

Everyone creates their own safety behaviours and so you have to identify what your own are. Some of the more popular safety behaviours include: not making eye contact, not engaging others, rehearsing in advance what you will say, avoiding small talk and monitoring every word said. Identifying your own safety behaviours is a tricky business. Perhaps you could think of a situation you have found difficult and then think about what you did to make yourself feel less vulnerable. Maybe you went to a party and stayed next to your partner all night. Maybe you feel the need to drink alcohol on a night out so you can talk wittily to others. Write a list of your own safety behaviours. Then begin to consider what is the worst that could happen if you stopped doing them? These thoughts will tend to be the ANTs associated with why you engage in this safety behaviour. Then move on to more balanced, rational thoughts to go with the safety behaviour.

For example, 'Small talk is not my favourite thing, but I am going to give it a try. After all it's not a Hollywood audition. I might even enjoy it'. Then test out your predictions by giving up your safety behaviours. You will find that over time, although at first it will be scary, you will become better at engaging in social situations and far less rigid and inflexible. Let me highlight this idea with one of my own examples. When I frequented the pub with my friends, the nature of our social encounters would be quick fire rapid banter. I found this type of humour and interaction difficult because of my social anxiety. I would become anxious, tense and nervous and I would remain quiet for the most part, skimming the periphery of the conversation. I would internalise and thus not really follow the conversation, but remember I was still desperate to be liked and to be social. I would therefore occasionally fire off a salvo of forced awkward jokes that were often ridiculous in their design and delivery. Often this would cause hilarious uproar amongst my friends bringing more negative focus on myself and so the cycle went on and on. To overcome this, I challenged many of the ANTs I had about socialising: 'I will have nothing to say', 'I'm boring' and so on.

I gave myself more realistic alternatives such as: 'socialising has been difficult in the past, but it's OK to make mistakes'; 'This isn't a Hollywood audition, I am going to relax and enjoy it'; 'I feel anxiety now, but no big deal I can cope with it'; 'The more I focus outward, the easier it will become'.

Then I identified my safety behaviours which were primarily: staying on the fringes of the conversation;

focusing on my own internal anguish losing track of the conversation; forcing myself to say something witty and drinking alcohol.

When I stopped drinking myself silly, and I stopped focusing internally, and I stopped staying on the periphery, and I stopped forcing out witty banter, I began to interact more easily. Consequently, my anxiety went down, my truer self came out and over time people began to respond to me differently. I had grabbed my courage and tried something new.

Sometimes you might try something new and the person doesn't react in the way you hoped. Maybe you begin to tell your friends more personal things or you begin to express opinions that you have been repressing because you believed you didn't have the right to one. Remember, you cannot control how people respond to you. They may look uninterested or even bored, but do not take this personally. It's easy to fall back into the traps of mind reading, taking things personally and all the other ANTS, but remember, you can only do your best and nothing more...then let it go. In my experience, when you stop avoiding, change your thinking processes and experiment with dropping your safety behaviours, people around you will relate to you increasingly more positively. As I began more socially successful, my life began to improve and this success brought more success: I had begun to change myself and the world around me.

Twelve: You are the creator

When we begin to change, the world around us changes too. It will seem less hostile and more of a place of opportunity and challenge. As you begin to change beliefs that you have long held about yourself from the point of view of a social anxiety suffer, your whole life will change too. You can actively work on attitudes and beliefs to help speed up your progress too. It is very true that you can create the world around you: you are the architect of your own reality.

I know this sounds far-fetched and pie in the sky kind of stuff but it's true. Consider the following examples. If you expect the world to be horrible, it will be. If you expect others to reject you, they will. If you believe you're not good enough for something, you won't be. You create expectations in your mind based on your beliefs and then you act upon these beliefs thus essentially making them happen. If you expect to be liked, you will be more outgoing and sociable. If you expect to enjoy a party, you will make the most of it. If you expect a date to like you, you will be more friendly and open (hey, she may not like you, but that's personal choice).

Many of us who are suffering from social anxiety view the world through a negative lens of social anxiety. We expect to fail. We expect to not make the grade. We see ourselves as different to everybody else. But let me be clear, there is nothing wrong with you. You are you and there is only one person like you. The only problem is you have been viewing the world through a broken lens and reacting accordingly. You have locked yourself into a downward, negative cycle that only you have the power to break free from. CBT is vital when we change this inaccurate belief system that we have created within ourselves. We need to re-think life because what you put into life you get back. If you put in negativity, you get it back. If you put in positivity, then you get it back.

When you begin to move away from your old beliefs, you will notice that people will slowly begin to react to you in a different, more positive way. Everyone in life has had negative events happen to them, and so have you but you now have a choice. On one hand, you can choose to worry, ruminate and live your life looking back in the rear view mirror wallowing in the past.

On the other hand, you can choose to change and move forward making progress. Your life starts today! If you believe you will get better, you will. If you believe that you can build inner strength, you will. If you believe that with every set back you will grow stronger, you will. If you believe it, it will happen. On my road to recovery, I had to radically change my viewpoint of the world. I wallowed in the emotional ruins of my anxiety day after day, but when I began the process of change, I moved forward and never stopped. If you are like me, you may want to learn some belief statements that you can say back to yourself every day for as long as you need to start viewing the world in a more accurate way. Feel free to create your own, but ones that worked for me were:

Who cares?
No big deal!
Why am I worrying about this?
Worrying is a waste of my time and energy!
Why make mountains out of mole hills?
I can deal with anything that comes my way.
I'm okay as I am.
You can only do you best, then forget about it.
Everyone makes mistakes.

The above short phrases to some might sound like pithy maxims and if you convince yourself they are...they will be. In fact, they are really powerful beliefs that will have real change on your mind and body. Someone could say that telling yourself things are 'awful, 'horrible' and 'unbearable' are throwaway comments, but we know better...we know the devastation they cause on mind and body. So what will you choose to believe?

As your core belief statements change, you will continue to improve your self-esteem and confidence. As a result, you will begin to act different and make different choices in all manner of situations. But what happens when we have life challenges that rise up to test our new more rational selves (weddings, speeches, interviews). The tendency is for us with social anxiety is begin to procrastinate and **worry.**

I was a worrier. I would worry about talking to strangers. I would worry about voicing an opinion. I would worry about making mistakes. I would worry about saying the wrong thing. I would worry about doing the right thing. I would worry about being worried. I would worry that I wasn't worried enough. I'm sure you get the theme. I had a belief: it was a strong and unwavering belief that worrying is positive and at the end of that worry rainbow there was a pot of gold; a solution to the problem I had at the time. Let be clear, worry is never positive. Worry is an ANT-like process. It will lead you in the wrong direction and try to frighten you. It blows things out of proportion, it exaggerates and it leaves a trail of anxiety and depression behind it. Worry will try to trick you into being irrational and it will promise that if you worry about something just a little more that you will come to a solution. The solution never comes. The process will rob you of minutes and hours of your day. To overcome social anxiety you must put a stop to worry. When you catch yourself ruminating about some future event, you must tell your brain to stop because you do have control over your thoughts. It might not be easy at first because breaking bad habits is never easy to do. I found it helpful when my mind began to spiral into worry to have some rational and well rehearsed statements at the ready. Once I said these statements to myself, I would focus away from the worry and think about something else or involve myself in another activity, thus keeping my mind off worrying.

Why am I worrying about this it's no big deal?
Nothing good ever came of worrying.
Worry is like a poison it will try and frighten me.
Why am I wasting my time worrying about this?
What will be will be.
Who cares?
Worrying is an ANT.

Like the Dali Lama said, "'If a problem is fixable, if a situation is such that you can do something about it, then there is no need to worry. If it's not fixable, then there is no help in worrying. There is no benefit in worrying whatsoever."

Thirteen: The enemy within

If you have reached this far in this book, congratulate yourself on a job well done. You have been resilient and triumphed over the geography that is my tale of woe, soon you will be able to plant your flag of exploration and maybe, just maybe, you may have learned something about yourself along the way. Hopefully, you now will have many skills to deal with social anxiety and your anxiety cycles have begun to shrink the more you use the strategies in this book. There is one final area of social anxiety in the quest for inner strength that I would like to explore, the idea of self-consciousness.

Self-consciousness comes when we focus our attention inward on our thoughts and feelings, and not externally on what is happening around us. It causes us to focus on our own internal struggle and at its worst can cause us to be paralysed in a social situation. For me, times such as entering a room full of people or saying goodbye to a host at the end of the party were the most difficult times as I knew I would be the centre of attention. I would rehearse what I might want to say. I would pressurise myself to say something memorable, something Oscar worthy that would dazzle the host with my dynamism. I would look inside myself constantly for answers in the outside world. I would over think it to the point of mental immobility. My self-consciousness, however, often was not contained to certain flash points, but could strike me at any point of a social interaction like Thor's hammer slamming down on my brain.

Self-consciousness doesn't stop at the brain though as it continues to ignite all the other tendrils of social anxiety: speeded up thinking, ANTs, physical sensations and safety behaviours. We then begin the very destructive process of checking in with our feelings and monitoring our anxiety levels. Self-monitoring has, in turn, a dual-pronged outcome. First, we begin to add fuel to the uncomfortable symptoms in our body as we give them more attention. Measuring your anxiety and wondering whether it will get better or worse, checking it with a mental thermometer guarantees it will stick around for longer. Second, we mistakenly assume these feelings to be reality and we become fearful others may notice this fear and we become increasingly fearful to how they may respond. As we become increasingly inward looking, the information we can assimilate from external sources begins to decline. If we do hear someone's conversation, it will tend to be muddled and inaccurate as we have left little mental processing power for this function. Studies have shown that socially anxious people tend to remember fewer details about social events than their non-socially anxious counterparts. Self-consciousness is something that requires time and effort to challenge, but if you believe you can get better, you will.

The secret to reducing self-consciousness is to focus on what is happening outside you rather than what is going on inside. Remember feelings inside your body often do not tell you the truth and can suck you into an internal struggle which will ultimately offer no solution. If you find yourself going inside yourself, then bring your attention back to the people around you. Be like a scientist and engage your curiosity of people. Listen carefully to what they are saying and doing. Be an interested observer.

I know this seems like common sense, but to us that suffer social anxiety, and definitely in my case, it was not. I would constantly be drifting internally and checking up on my thoughts and feelings. Often, I would make a comment that wasn't relevant to the conversation much to the hilarity of others.

Self-consciousness is ultimately a safety behaviour. It allows you to escape inside yourself and thus escape the fear in the world around you namely getting involved too deeply with others. This strategy is ultimately flawed as it prevents you from seeing you can actually cope when interacting with other people. I had to work diligently on being able to catch myself from turning my focus inside. How did I do it? The best way to decrease self-consciousness is, like I said earlier, to focus on the person and be curious. Your goal is to increase the time spent externally focusing and minimising the time spent internally focus. At the same time, we are only human and our attention will wax and wane...this is totally normal. What is not normal is when internal focus outweighs external to the detriment of your ability to communicate effectively. Attention is a dynamic system that will be changing and moving; it will move back to an internal focus. When this happens, you have to catch yourself and turn your attention back out into the environment around you. Don't deny the opportunity of accumulating information from the outside world when you are socialising.

Fourteen: It's my life

When I was in the depths of social anxiety, my greatest dream was to be 'normal': to be able to interact with people and engage in the world in a meaningful way. Am I normal now? Perhaps it would be apt to answer this question with another question, is anybody truly normal? Some would say I am normal and some, I'm sure, would say I'm not. But who cares? Like the poet, John Lydgate, said, 'You can please some of the people all of the time, you can please all of the people some of the time, but you can't please all of the people all of the time.'

I spent too much of my life worrying about what people thought of me. I accept myself as I am and through acceptance freedom comes. At my social anxiety's worst, I suffered from panic disorder, suicidal thoughts and I was house bound due to debilitating agoraphobia. I lost relationships and pushed friends from my life. My career stalled and floundered. I was dosed up on drugs and was close to being sectioned under the Mental Health Act. So where am I now?

Thanks to CBT I have made a full recovery and I would now say that due to persistence with the ideas and concepts in this book, I have an above average level of confidence. My career has been solid and successful. I have a good group of friends that I have had since childhood and so they stood the test of my affliction. Are some of my good friends disappointed that I didn't attend significant dates in our shared lives such as holidaying together, most probably. Am I worried about the affect social anxiety has had on my life...not really. The thing with social anxiety is that it tries very hard to destroy your life, but once you have uncovered its game and you have started your journey of recovery, you have to leave the past behind.

For us, the idea that you can't live your life looking in the rear view mirror is so important. I don't worry about choices I have made in the past; I simply accept them, let them go and move forward. If you have any negative experiences or thoughts from the past and they are weighing you down today, let it be free and let it go. All the shame, negativity and suffering from the past can have no hold on you today unless you let it. Don't choose to wallow in the mistakes of the past as no answers can be found there. The past is a foreign country; they do things differently there. Start to live your life differently and you will be able to treat others around you with love, kindness, and caring that you never thought possible in the midst of social anxiety.

And so, I let it all go and I move through life calmly and confidently. I am now 5 years free of social anxiety. I have a beautiful partner, good friends and a newborn son; there's nothing to hold me back; there's nothing to hold you back.

Fifteen: Helpful tit-bits

During my recovery from social anxiety, I have come across many useful lifestyle changes that I thought would be worthwhile to share. Feel free to use these ideas to supplement the CBT in this book, all of them I found hugely beneficial to support my recovery.

Exercise

For anybody suffering from social anxiety, exercise is a great tool for relieving stress and promoting physical and mental health. Numerous studies have shown exercise to increase mood through boosting neurotransmitters such as endorphins and serotonin. Further, simply getting outside into the fresh air can elevate mood and make us feel good. To support my recovery, I would make sure I excised at least fifteen minutes every day in the morning. I didn't exercise to the point of exhaustion, but I made sure that I was gently working my body and starting the day with fresh air and bird song. It really does make a difference!

Diet

For the human body to function properly it needs a steady stream of nutrients so it can create the neurotransmitters needed to regulate mood and manage anxiety. I made sure that I cleaned up my diet, cutting out all processed foods and eating plenty of fruit and vegetables. Also I made sure my gut bacteria was healthy by taking in weekly probiotic drinks which are available from any supermarket. Probiotics aid in the digestion of food and therefore the absorption of nutrients. I also cut out all sweetened beverages (fruit juices, fizzy drinks) as studies have shown that such drinks can lead to an increase in depression.

Cutting out beverages brings me onto caffeine. For me, cutting out caffeine from your diet, or at least reducing it, is an important step when overcoming social anxiety. Caffeine works by blocking the depressant function of adenosine. Caffeine thus can increase alertness, concentration and memory but drinking too much can increase the stimulating properties of the drug ending up in sweaty palms and a racing heart. During my recovery, I cut out caffeine completely, but now, admittedly, I do partake in moderation, safe in the knowledge that if I am a bit jittery after a cup, that it is the tea and nothing else.

The problem I found was when I was suffering from anxiety, I would have a cup of coffee with my friends, begin to feel jittery and then attribute the anxiety to the social situation thus increasing my overall anxiety of social situations. A last point of note when we are thinking about caffeine would be to mention that you should stay away from energy drinks at all costs. In a study in the Journal of Anxiety and Depression, over 1000 20-year-olds, who drank at least one 8.4-ounce energy drink a day reported higher anxiety. The more energy drinks they consume, the more chronic and frequent the anxiety became. There's a reason why taurine, an active ingredient in energy drinks, has been banned in a number of

European countries. In conclusion, it may, depending on your point of recovery, be worthwhile looking at your caffeine intake.

Alcohol

Alcohol is a depressant and for my social anxiety it had no helpful properties whatsoever. If you suffer from an anxiety disorder, the quickest way to recovery is by eliminating alcohol from your diet. There are a number of problems with drinking that are unhelpful to somebody with social anxiety such as robbing the body of important nutrients and damaging bodily functions. But perhaps the greatest problem is, whether we are aware of it or not, alcohol is one of the biggest safety behaviours going.

Drinking alcohol prevents us from exploring social situations and teaching ourselves that we can cope in them and we can be social people. For example, if we get drunk and the social occasion goes well, the mind attributes this to the social lubricating properties of the alcohol. Alcohol is great at keeping us trapped in negative social anxiety pathways and hinders our recovery. If you remove alcohol from the equation and continue to follow the CBT in this book, you will recover more quickly.

Sleep

When we don't sleep well, it can have a significant impact on your mood. During sleep, our brain is replenishing our neurotransmitters which are linked to good mood and so getting our eight hours a night while following our CBT and other lifestyle changes can be a helpful tool in our anxiety defeating tool box.

Sixteen: Useful organisations

The following organisations offer help and support to sufferers of social anxiety as well as other mental-health issues.

Samaritans

Samaritan's provide 24 hour support which is confidential. They help people suffering from despair and anxiety. You can contact them by email, phone, text or face to face. If you feel upset or confused, the Samaritans can help you.

Phone:
08457 90 90 90

Web Site:
http://www.samaritans.org

Anxiety UK

Established in 1970, this national charity

provides support to anybody suffering from anxiety.

Phone:
08444 775 774

Web Site:
http://www.anxietyuk.org.uk/

Breathing Space

Breathing space is a confidential phone line where you can discusses anything that is causing you distress such as: exam pressure, relationship problems and so on.

Phone:
0800 83 85 87

Web Site:

http://www.breathingspacescotland.co.uk

Living Life to the Full

An online life skills course made up of several different modules designed to help develop key skills and tackle some of the problems we all face from time to time.

Web Site:
http://www.llttf.com/

Thank you for buying my book. I hope that by reading my story, you have been inspired to make a change in your life. If this book helps just one person like me, then it has been a total success. If you thought it was helpful, then recommend it to a friend or family member because in the world of social anxiety knowledge truly is power. Please review my book on Amazon; I would love to hear your feedback.

Feel free to contact me at my website

www.myanxietyandme.com

Regards,

Peter